A WRITER'S NOTEBOOK

The Ultimate Guide to
Creative Writing

A WRITER'S NOTEBOOK

The Ultimate Guide to Creative Writing

Pamela Curtis Swallow

SCHOLASTIC INC.
New York Toronto London Auckland Sydney
Mexico City New Delhi Hong Kong

ISBN 0-590-14969-5

Cover and interior design by Louise Bova

12 11 10 9 8 7 6 5 4 3 2 1   9/9 0 1 2 3 4/0

Printed in the U.S.A.   40

First Scholastic printing, September 1999

A WRITER'S NOTEBOOK

The Ultimate Guide to Creative Writing

This notebook is a place to enjoy writing and to grow as a writer. Don't be critical of yourself. Your ideas are as good as anyone's. In time, you will find your own writing voice. You are unique and you don't need to try to sound like anyone but yourself.

Your notebook will become a treasure chest of ideas for more writing. Some of your notes and ideas may take time before they are ready to be developed. They'll be like bread dough rising or kernels of corn popping. Ideas that may seem small at first may develop into whole stories, dramatic scenes, and page-turning chapter endings.

You'll learn to write well by writing often. Write what pleases *you*. You are your most important audience. This notebook is a place for you to write because you *want* to, not because you *have* to. As a writer, you can choose to put whatever you wish in your notebook. There are no rules.

So relax, smile, give yourself a thumbs-up, and go to it. This writing is for *you*.

Why write?

Three reasons might be:

- ☆ To catch what's bubbling and bursting inside of you and get it down on paper.

- ☆ To learn more about yourself.

- ☆ To become a better observer.

What other reasons can you think of?

To let your imgination run wild
+ Do everything you wouldn't
be able to do in real world.

Some writers write because they like to explore and investigate. *What do you suppose they might be looking for?*

What writing tools do writers need?

Each writer is different. And many use more than one tool. Some writers swear by a pencil and a pad. They like the feel of the pencil in their hand and its movement across the paper. Others like a ballpoint or fountain pen. There are writers who love the clickety sound of a typewriter and others who are devoted to their computers.

But because one thing is important to all writers . . . **seizing the moment** . . . most make it a habit to carry a small notebook, a few index cards, or even a miniature tape recorder to capture observations and ideas right away. Lots of times we read, see, or hear something that makes us laugh, cry, or want to investigate. We think we'll remember it later, but that doesn't always happen. Things slip away; they get buried under other things. The best way to keep hold of things we want to remember is to record them right away.

How do writers start, anyway?

Slowly, with one word . . . then another. One sentence . . . then another. One paragraph . . . then another. Before you know it — PRESTO! POOF! POP! You'll have a story.

When should you write?

Don't wait around for the perfect time and place to write. Train yourself to write *any* time and *any* place.

When you first wake up . . . at a desk . . . up a tree . . . while on a bus . . . under a table . . . in a leaf pile . . . waiting in the dentist's office . . . on a rock . . . in a car . . . with your pet . . . in the bathtub . . . in a closet . . . under your bedcovers before you sleep.

Should you date each piece of writing?

That's up to you. Some writers like to keep track of their ideas and their growth as writers. Others prefer to take a relaxed approach. Each writer is different. And each has an individual way of working. This includes you. You may get tips and ideas from other writers, but in the end, you will have your *own* unique style. That's as it should be.

What about inspiration?

Author Jack London said, "You can't wait for inspiration. You have to go after it with a club." He's telling us that we shouldn't sit back and wait for "The Inspiration Fairy" to whisper in our ear. We have to take action, be alert, and be determined to make our writing happen.

Where do writers get ideas?

Professional writers do not have magic pots in which to brew ideas, or special traps with which to catch ideas, or extra powerful antennae for hearing ideas. They live in the same world as everyone else . . . but they **pay attention**. They keep their "idea receptors" turned on and tuned in.

Writers are observers.

And ideas are everywhere: in the tree outside your window, under your great-aunt Tillie's bed, in a bug's ear, under a log, and stuck to your refrigerator with a magnet. Tune in and you'll notice them.

Some writers notice interesting stories and articles in the news and get ideas that way; often they keep a file collection of these news pieces. Here's a curious tidbit that was in a major New Jersey newspaper:

> Garden tip: Give Juicy Fruit gum to woodchucks. They will eat the gum and not return. Unwrap the sticks of gum and leave them where woodchucks have been feeding.

Now, crank up your imagination and have some fun with this information. Imagine that it was your job to check with the woodchucks to see what kinds of gum they liked and didn't like. How did you get this job as tester of woodchuck gum preferences? How did the woodchucks act when offered Bubblicious? Bazooka bubble gum? Did they come back for more? How did they feel about Dentyne? Were they worried about attracting attention with fresh, white teeth and flashy smiles? Put yourself in the place of a woodchuck — why would you go away and not come back after having a stick of Juicy Fruit?

And here's another newspaper story that might be "expandable" into something more:

> *The great white shark is a finicky eater. Humans may actually cause indigestion. This is why humans are so often released after being attacked.*

Suppose you try to think like a shark with a sensitive stomach. Do other kinds of sharks make fun of you? Are you upset about ruining your reputation as the meanest and scariest of all sharks? What would make you happy? Write about this.

_____

_____

_____

_____

_____

_____

_____

_____

_____

_____

See what news stories you can find that might grow into something more. Use this space to glue or tape your articles and to jot down your story ideas.

_____
_____
_____
_____
_____
_____
_____
_____
_____
_____
_____
_____
_____
_____
_____
_____

Here's a real, but curious, "For Sale" item from a local paper:

Gnomes for sale.
72 gnomes, many retired.
Value approx. $8,500.
Will sacrifice.
Serious inquiries only.

What kind of story might grow from
that advertisement? Who or what are those gnomes?
What did they do before they retired? Are they related
to one another? Who is selling them and why? How do
the gnomes feel about it? What happens next?

_____

_____

_____

_____

_____

_____

_____

See if you can find a "For Sale" ad that makes you
wonder. You can invent a whole story to explain why
the item is being sold, who is selling it, who is buying
it, and what happens next.

Writers don't just pay attention to things they see, they also listen.

Have you ever caught part of other people's interesting conversation when you were walking past them? Or have you overheard someone on the telephone saying something intriguing? It makes you want to know what's going on, doesn't it? It makes you want to fill in the blanks so you'll know the whole story.

Just suppose you were walking by a young man who's at a pay phone and you hear him say, "Throw it on the table and see if it bounces."

Expand this little peculiar remark and fill in some blanks. Who's saying, "Throw it on the table and see if it bounces"? Who's he speaking to? What would be thrown? Why care if it bounces? What happens if it does? What if it doesn't?

_____

_____

_____

_____

Writers collect.

They collect words, places, faces, names, sounds, characters, what ifs, wonderings, and whys. It's satisfying to have such collections to pull from when you need something for a piece of writing.

Writing depends upon words — the right ones.

So let's begin with a word collection. What are some words you especially like? Some may sound nice to you, or make you think of something particular. A word collection contains cozy words, scary words, angry words, funny words, gentle words, snappy words, serious words, tough words, all sorts of words.

Some examples might be:

persnickety	riffle	fob
doughy	snuggle-bugger	pincer
positutely	shuck	wizened
nudge	quiver	marmalade

Add some favorite words of your own and keep a watch out for wonderful words to keep your collection growing.

You can collect memories — essential writing material.

For example: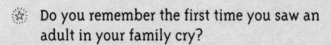

- ☆ Do you remember the first time you saw an adult in your family cry?

- ☆ Do you remember your first day ever of school?

- ☆ Your most embarrassing moment?

- ☆ When your best friend was really angry at you?

Describe some memories, using as many details as you can. You may find that some memories are so rich that you'll feel like a miner who's struck gold.

_____

_____

_____

_____

_____

_____

_____

_____

Sometimes a phrase or single sentence will come to you — one of those kernels that eventually PRESTO! POOF! POPS! into a full-blown story. You can begin a collection of such lines.

Here are a few to start you off:

☆ The smell of feet was overpowering.

☆ She missed her chance.

☆ This is one journey you have to make alone.

☆ Peanut butter and tuna fish sandwich

☆ He's afraid to jump.

☆ Gum in my hair on class picture day

Your special phrases and sentences just might be like magic beans that sprout and grow... and grow... and grow.

Did you ever think of collecting faces?

You'll be glad you did when you need an interesting character for a story. Here's one way to start your collection: Find a photograph in a newspaper or magazine of someone you think looks interesting. Rather than reading what's already written about this person, create a life from your imagination for this person. Try having an imaginary "talk" with this person, asking lots of questions and getting to know what's important to him or her. Then write what you think has already happened in his or her life. You might very well end up with a memorable character for a story.

_____

_____

_____

_____

_____

_____

_____

_____

A collection of hopes is valuable when you need writing ideas.

For example:

☆ What do you hope your next year of school will be like?

☆ Who do you hope will be your best friend always?

☆ What do you hope your house will be like when you grow up?

☆ What do you hope will stop happening to you?

☆ What discoveries do you hope will be made soon?

_____

_____

_____

_____

_____

_____

_____

_____

_____

"What ifs" are great story starters.

Many writers use them to *rev up* their imaginations.

- ☆ What if that egg you're cracking to make pancakes contains a live platypus?

- ☆ What if the lawn chair you're relaxing on floats up into the sky?

- ☆ What if your minty green toothpaste turns your teeth minty green?

- ☆ What if you woke up with Minnie Mouse feet?

- ☆ What if your math teacher needs those scarves she always wears to hold her head on?

You can make up your own "what ifs," or use the ones above to expand into stories.

_____

_____

_____

_____

_____

_____

As a writer, once you start collecting, you'll become very observant. You'll notice names on trucks, faces and phrases on billboards, colors in advertisements, smells in cafeterias, textures of cloth, and noises on the street.

You'll sharpen your people-watching skills.

A young woman might sit near you on a bus, and you'll notice all sorts of things about her: what kind of jewelry she has, how worn her jeans look, that her baseball cap is hiding messy hair, that she's reading a science magazine . . . You'll wonder where she grew up, where she's going, what she likes to do, and why she looks as if she's been crying.

You can practice a more detailed exercise by taking a look at a person you often see but barely know — perhaps the person who delivers your mail or works at a nearby gas station. First write what you observe: how your person dresses, moves, talks — and whether your person seems comfortable, happy, relaxed, and so on. Include as many details as you can.

Then expand this and use your imagination. Where do you suppose this person grew up and what was his or her family like? What was the family money situation? What was this person like at your age? What was school like for this person and who were his or her friends? Were there any pets? What were this person's favorite things to do? What were this person's secrets? What habits did this person have? How about fears? What did this person want more than anything? What did he or she expect to become as a grown-up?

And now — what do you suppose this person's life is like? Family? What plans do you think this person might have? Is your person happy? Why or why not?

When you are done, you will have done the same kind of work an author does to develop a character for a story.

_____

_____

_____

_____

_____

_____

_____

_____

_____

_____

_____

_____

Letters

Some important writing is done in this form. Choose someone to write to who is no longer alive — perhaps Abraham Lincoln, your great-grandmother, your first pet, Martin Luther King, Jr., or Elvis. In your letter, you could tell about your life, about changes, and about things you wish you could talk over with this person.

When you are finished, write a letter back to yourself from this person. You may decide to learn more about this person before writing, so that the letter sounds authentic.

You could do this with a friend. You could be one famous dead person, your friend another. Now write to each other. Have fun with the possibilities: Martin Luther King, Jr., carrying on a correspondence with Abraham Lincoln, or perhaps Elvis and Helen Keller as pen pals.

Have you ever been to a family reunion or large family gathering? Lots of writing material there!

☆ You can describe how different relatives looked and dressed.

☆ Are there any family traits you noticed? A particular nose, chin, eyes, or laugh?

☆ Which family members seemed to get the most respect? Any idea why?

☆ What family recipes did you taste? What were they like? Are there any "famous" ones that weren't actually all that well liked and, in fact, made a few family dogs sick under the table?

☆ What family stories were told? Grab onto these tales!

_____

_____

_____

_____

_____

_____

Fill up the following blank space with things you wonder about. Who knows, these little things might puff up into something bigger.

Here are a few to start you off:

☆ Why are people who are scared called chickens?

☆ Why aren't dimes bigger than nickels?

☆ If teachers scold out-of-control classes for being "unruly," why aren't well-behaved classes complimented for being "ruly"?

☆ When you look up into the night sky and make a wish, is anyone or anything up there looking down on Earth and wishing on us?

_____

_____

_____

_____

_____

_____

_____

_____

free writing

It's helpful to free your mind by spending some time every day *free writing* — putting down on paper whatever comes into your mind. Don't worry about what comes out, whether it makes sense, if one thought relates to the next, or if your spelling and grammar are correct — just write. Any and all topics will do.

Your free writing could go something like this:

That movie last night was pretty good, except that I got tired of sitting on that chair, and the woman in front of me had on some nasty perfume, so I stuck my nose into my Junior Mints box. The music was creepy — I bet I wouldn't have been half as scared if they'd used a kazoo instead of a cello. A kazoo is never taken seriously. Who decides things like that? Is there a list that matches musical instruments to moods like sadness, suspense, and excitement? What kind of instrument would I use right now to go with all these questions? . . . (and so on.)

Just let your mind go free and write.

"Think writing"

This can be done anywhere — in the shower, at your locker, during a school assembly program, staring out a window, waiting for your soccer game to begin . . . wherever you are. When you're "think writing," you're coming up with names, ideas, lines of dialogue — and since you don't want these things to slip away, the sooner you get them down on paper the better. Use this space for your "think writing" ideas.

_____

_____

_____

_____

_____

_____

_____

_____

_____

_____

_____

Experimenting with writing

It's interesting to see what happens when you try new things. For example, put on your favorite piece of "feel-good music" and free write for ten minutes.
Then switch the music and put on something more somber and serious-sounding and free write for ten more minutes. In what ways have mood and sound affected your writing?

Here's another kind of experiment:

Try writing from a different vantage point than you usually have, perhaps under the kitchen table, where you can get a pet's-eye or bug's-eye view of things. What are you seeing, hearing, and smelling? What does the underside of the table look like? If your pet or a bug were doing the writing, what do you suppose would be said?

How about under your bed? In a garage? On your belly in the grass?

Or find a high spot and write from up there, where you have a bird's-eye view.

Pretend you are a visitor from a far-off place and you are seeing a carnival or circus for the first time. Really notice details and write about this event as if you're recording it all for the "folks back home."

Photographs can be a good source of ideas.

See if you can find one taken of you three or four years ago. Can you describe what it was like to be you then? Can you imagine what you'll be like ten years from now?

Perhaps you can find a photograph of a parent or grandparent when they were young. Can you describe how they looked and what you imagine they might have been like at that age?

Study a photograph of someone famous and see if you can get inside his or her head. You might like to choose a favorite TV or movie personality. Imagine what it would be like to really *be* that person. Write about the day that this personality learns of his or her "big break" into the world of show biz.

Dreams are wonderful springboards for writing!

For example:

- ☆ Suppose you had a dream about the Loch Ness lobster?

- ☆ Or about the hamster that ate Pittsburgh?

- ☆ How about the revenge of the veggie burgers?

- ☆ Or the gym teacher whose ears flew off when he blew his whistle too hard?

Think of a dream you've had, sprinkle it with your creative juices, and cook up a story.

_____

_____

_____

_____

_____

_____

_____

Questions

Lots of writing comes from questions: What? Where? Why? Who? How? Do you suppose?

Here's an example: You are driving past the site where your new school is being built, and you see a *huge* lump covered with dark plastic sheeting. Out of the corner of your eye, you think you see the lump move.

- ☆ What is it and is it alive?

- ☆ Where is it from? Where is it going to live? (Under the school?)

- ☆ Why is it there?

- ☆ Who else knows about it?

- ☆ How are you going to find out more about that eerie thing?

- ☆ Do you suppose it dances with the construction equipment under the full moon?

- ☆ Did *it* see *you* see *it*?

- ☆ Will it still be there on the first day of school?

Continue with more questions until you have the makings of a wacky, wonderful story. Go to it!

Three story starters — help yourself!

I couldn't move. I just stood there staring at the audience and feeling sick.

It was fun to imagine that my pets could talk. I pretended that they said some pretty humorous things. But what Snuffles said, I mean <u>really</u> said, last night made the hairs on my neck stand up.

The school bus dropped me off at the end of my driveway. I walked to the house and opened the front door. Facing me in the living room were my parents, my grandfather, and my older brother. "We have something we have to talk with you about," my father said.

_____

_____

_____

_____

_____

_____

_____

_____

Chocolate chip cookies? Maybe!

When you take a recipe card for your great-grand-mother's chocolate chip cookies and you follow the directions, adding all the right ingredients, you can feel confident that what comes out of the oven will be wonderful (and appreciated by all). Does a recipe for a story work out as predictably?

Let's imagine:

sugar = main character
eggs = other characters
flour = setting
baking soda = plot
salt = problem
butter = story flow
vanilla = point of view
nuts = dialogue
chocolate chips = solution to the problem

You "mix as if you mean it" (because those are your great-grandmother's exact words), bake in the oven . . . and . . . ta-da! You *thought* you'd have the predictably perfect and delicious story. After all, you had all the right ingredients. But it doesn't work that way with writing; there are surprises. Your story's development won't be as predictable as your cookies.

Is that so bad? Not at all — it's interesting.

LET'S LOOK AT WHAT GOES INTO A STORY. . .

Beginnings

Your story should start immediately in order to snag the reader. Don't dillydally getting to the point. You don't have to come out and state the main character's problem right off, but you'll want the reader to at least sense it.

Beginnings can be tricky. If you're not sure how to start your story, just begin it anyway. You may find that the place where you first start ends up not being your real opening after all. But that's okay. It happens to lots of writers. Sometimes you need to work on getting to know your characters and their problems before you know how to write that first-page "grabber." Some writers wait until they've worked out their ending before they finally settle on their beginning. The beginning and the end balance each other. Knowing one helps to know the other.

Here are some ways you can start:

With dialogue:

"That's the last straw — you're a big creep!" Freddy shouted.

With an introduction by the main character:
I'm not a calm person. That's how I got the nickname Freddy the Firecracker.

With description:
Freddy's report card had no white space. Every inch of it was filled with teachers' comments about his need to control his temper.

With a question:
What kind of shrimpy sixth-grader would insult the hugest boy in the eighth grade?

With background material:
Since the time Freddy was old enough to mix with other kids, his feisty personality got him into fixes.

Characters

You can't have a story without them! They're what makes things happen.

Each character you create comes *through* you and *from* you. In writing about characters' emotions, opinions, and struggles, you'll learn a lot about your own. Your characters will teach you about yourself.

When you write about a character, it is important to know what the character wants. There has to be a reason for behavior. Another word for this is **motive**. You hear a lot about motive in mystery and crime stories, but "suspicious characters" aren't the only ones with motives.

First we decide what our characters want and then we make it hard for them to get it. A character without a problem isn't very interesting.

You want your main character to be likable but not perfect. Think back to *The Tale of Peter Rabbit*. Were you interested in the "good little bunnies" — Flopsy, Mopsy, and Cottontail — or were you interested in Peter?

Your character should be believable, flaws and all.

☆ Does your character tend to exaggerate?

☆ Does your character hide bad test papers?

☆ Does your character giggle uncontrollably at the wrong times?

☆ Does your character leap before looking?

Just as you must know what your main character wants, you must also know what your "villain" wants. Why is the villain behaving a certain way? How far will the villain go to get what he or she wants? What's at stake?

Remember, just as the main character shouldn't be *all* good, the villain shouldn't be *all* bad.

Developing your character

Many writers do this before they start their story. Decide who your main character will be and then begin to build this person a life. Be thorough in building a **character profile**:

- ☆ Character's name and age
- ☆ Where and when the story takes place
- ☆ Character's parents and what they're like
- ☆ Character's sisters and brothers and what they're like
- ☆ Character's pets and how important they are in the family
- ☆ Character's friends and what they're like
- ☆ What the character looks like
- ☆ What the character likes to wear
- ☆ What the character likes to eat
- ☆ Description of the character's bedroom
- ☆ What secrets are hidden and where
- ☆ What the character is embarrassed by
- ☆ What the character is afraid of
- ☆ What negative traits the character has
- ☆ The character's conflict/struggle/problem
- ☆ What it is that the character wants more than anything
- ☆ The way the character will change and grow
- ☆ What it is that will make the reader care about the character

More about your characters

Your main character will change as he or she deals with problems and struggles. You will have to decide how. Will your character start to feel differently? Accept something he or she hadn't been able to deal with? Overcome physical obstacles? It's up to you.

You will want to know your other characters, not just your main one. You'll need to know details about each of them. That way you'll understand how they fit into your main character's world. But since the story is not from their point of view, you will not have to go quite so far "inside" of them.

"Listen" to your characters and hear each of their unique voices. Try having a dialogue with them. Hear them speak and try to understand why they act and sound as they do. What do they tell you? What **body language** do they use? (What do they reveal about themselves through facial expressions, tone of voice, gestures, and other physical actions?)

See what happens when you let your characters have freedom to do and say what they wish. Step aside and let the characters "live" in the story. They'll tell you what should happen next.

Character tags

These are ways we distinguish and identify characters — ways that make them distinct individuals.

For example:

- ☆ Biting his nails
- ☆ Snorting when she laughs
- ☆ Wrinkling his nose to move his glasses up
- ☆ Having a squeaky little sneeze
- ☆ Gazing upward when she's thinking
- ☆ Dabbing cover-up stick on her pimples

Think of character tags that you can use in your writing and list them here.

_____

_____

_____

_____

_____

_____

_____

_____

Non human characters

Not all characters are people. Many are animals and some are even inanimate objects.

For fun, try writing about the thoughts and feelings of a "thing":

- ☆ Your refrigerator
- ☆ Your family car
- ☆ Your pink eraser
- ☆ Your brother's toothbrush
- ☆ Your teacher's wastebasket

_____

_____

_____

_____

_____

_____

_____

_____

_____

Write about what you know

Readers are hardly ever fooled by a writer *pretending* to know about something. This is why writers are advised to write about what they know. This applies both to story subject matter and to setting. The **setting** is where and when your story takes place. It's important that you feel comfortable there: that it's either a place and time you know well or have researched carefully. If you don't feel "at home" in the setting, your reader won't feel drawn in and comfortable, either.

What subjects and places do you know a lot about?

Movies?   Boston?
Skating?   Your neighborhood?
Gerbils?   Your grandparents' home?
Baby-sitting?   Summer camp?

Make a list of things you feel that you could write about with confidence.

_____

_____

_____

_____

_____

Most fiction writers begin with **real-life material**, such as events that really happened, people they really knew, or feelings they really had. Then they mold the material to suit their story. How? They adjust, rearrange, tone down, and crank up. They often make things "more" — more tense, more funny, more dramatic, more romantic, more sad, more settled.

The "truth" is rearranged and transformed. Character traits of many people writers know become "mixed and matched," blended and disguised. It is as if you dropped a picture made from mosaic tiles . . . and then you picked up the tiles and fit them together differently, but still you created a picture.

Choose a photograph of a person from a magazine or newspaper. Write a description of this person's personality and life by selecting traits of different people you have known. The blend you come up with will be a unique character, yet familiar to you in so many ways.

_____

_____

_____

_____

_____

_____

_____

_____

Details

Wherever you can, be precise. Your reader gets a richer picture from your description.

Instead of *fish* write *flounder* (which looks nothing like a trout or a catfish).

Rather than say that a *bird* is flying overhead, say *swallow*, if that's the kind you mean — the image of a swallow swooping and soaring playfully in the air is a distinct image — you wouldn't want your reader imagining a buzzard or a grackle.

Dinner doesn't give us the same picture as spaghetti with mushroom sauce, salad, garlic bread, and coffee ice cream.

You don't have to search for fancy long words. Strong simple words work just fine. Just make them precise and if possible *authentic* — that means you will be describing something you've truly observed.

For example, instead of just saying *teacher's desk* and leaving it at that, describe a teacher's desk you've really seen, complete with the coffee-stained blotter, the lesson plan book, the calendar highlighting all the school holidays, the pages of morning announcements from the office, the list of overdue library books owed by kids in the class, a photograph of the teacher's children, and maybe a bottle of aspirin in the middle drawer.

Details are important in your writing, but use thought in selecting them. Beware of "detail overload." Too much detail can be tiresome to read and can slow down your story.

Here's an example of perhaps more detail than necessary:

> *Emily opened her big baby-blue eyes and fluttered her long dark brown lashes as she sighed ever-so-softly and slowly raised her pale, thin arms to her head and brushed her orange-tinted "desert sunrise" hair off her broad forehead and then picked up her antique brass call-bell to summon Rex, the six-foot, three-and-a-half-inch-tall, "salt and pepper" gray-haired butler with the slight limp, which was the result of a rather embarrassing boyhood bowling accident.*

Now, with your pencil, cross out the unnecessary details.

For fun, take yourself and your notebook on a "**detail hunt**" and come back with a collection of all sorts of interesting details and observations.

For example:

☆ Your front porch

☆ Your grandfather's shoes

☆ Inside your dog's mouth

☆ Your first-grade school picture

☆ The tree by your bedroom window

☆ Your favorite pajamas

Now, think about your school lunchroom. Close your eyes for a moment and recall as many details as possible (even that hot doggy smell!). Open your eyes and write.

Here are some details you might include:

☆ Who sits where?

☆ What are the *cool* things to have in your lunch?

☆ What comments are usually made?

☆ Who's in charge?

☆ What are the smells?

☆ What do you hear?

☆ What does the floor feel like?

☆ What kinds of threats and bribes are used to keep control?

Senses

These are some of your best details. You want your reader to "experience" what it is you're writing about. One way to be sure this happens is to include sensory details.

Take your notebook outside — for a walk, for a bus ride, for a trip to the park, for a window-shopping stroll downtown. What do you see? Hear? Smell? Taste? Touch? Notice? Perk up those ears, open those eyes, and pay attention.

Remember a birthday party — either yours or someone else's — record as many sensory details as you can.

- ☆ The sounds of anticipation, preparation, guests, games, party poopers, singing, laughter

- ☆ The smells of pizza, candles, balloons, fruit punch

- ☆ The feel of presents, goody bags, paper hats, a full stomach

- ☆ The taste of cake, ice cream, candy

- ☆ The sight of decorations, sparkling eyes, spills, camera flashes

Some other suggestions for writing sensory details:

- ☆ Shopping for back-to-school supplies
- ☆ A *long* family car ride
- ☆ A hospital visit
- ☆ A hike in the woods
- ☆ Riding on a subway train

_____

_____

_____

_____

_____

_____

_____

_____

_____

_____

_____

_____

_____

_____

Strong words

Try to pick the most solid, precise words you can and leave them to stand on their own.

Some people think that by adding words such as *very*, *really*, *quite*, and *pretty* the meaning becomes stronger — usually the opposite is true. You're better off saying what you mean and standing behind it. If you don't have strong verbs and nouns, all the adverbs and adjectives in the world won't help.

Look at this sentence:

> *I really think I am quite lucky to be a pretty talented athlete.*

Now strengthen it by removing the words that add nothing.

Here's another one:

> *I feel extremely certain that the very last remark was a rather big mistake.*

Remove the words that weaken the sentence.

Show, don't tell.

You want your readers to "be there" as events are happening in your writing and to feel as though they are in the midst of the action. How do you do that? You "show" rather than "tell."

"Showing" means that you invite your readers to enter your story by allowing them to see and feel the events unfolding. You let them "feel" with the characters and don't merely let them know that the characters felt something. The readers have front-row orchestra seats and can experience the drama along with the characters.

"Telling" means that you let the readers know about things after they have happened or without letting the reader "watch" the action. The reader "hears" about something that happened but does not experience it. The reader is kept at a distance outside the story. You've stuck them way back in the cheap seats, far removed from your drama.

For example:

Telling:
Janet was shocked by what Dennis asked her.
(You've told the reader how the character felt.)
Showing:
It was as if someone had punched all the breath out of Janet. Her face was turning either red or white, she couldn't tell which. She felt hot and cold at the same time. Her answer was stuck somewhere between her brain and her throat. She just stared at Dennis.
(You've shown the reader how the character felt.)

Practice showing and not telling by writing two examples of your own for each.

Body language

Body language is a form of "showing" rather than "telling" something about the character. It is used to suggest a character's mood or state of mind. Facial expressions, tone of voice, gestures, and other physical actions tell us a lot about a character.

For example:

- ☆ If a girl continues to nervously twist her hair around her finger when she's being scolded, the reader can conclude that she's anxious or upset, even though the author doesn't come right out and say it.

- ☆ Disgust can be shown when a character sticks his finger down his throat and pretends to gag.

- ☆ Tapping a foot or tapping a finger on a tabletop suggests impatience.

Such gestures give added depth and dimension to a character. Body language is a powerful writing device because the reader often experiences the same physical feelings as the character.

In a brief scene, describe how a girl acted when called to the principal's office. Include a generous sprinkling of body language.

Point of view

This tells us where the story is coming from and who's telling it. The most common point of view is that of the main character. This is the person whose head and skin we are generally in.

In **first person**, the main character tells the story and refers to himself or herself as "I." For example:

> *My name is Katy Randall and I just had my eleventh birthday. I am in Mr. Damiano's sixth-grade class at Eleanor Roosevelt Middle School.*

Earlier in your writer's notebook, there was a suggested exercise in which you were asked to write letters. If you turn back to page 29, you will find this. You may not have realized it then, but you were practicing writing in the first person.

Another way to become comfortable with writing in the first person is to try writing entries in an imaginary diary or journal of another person. This person could be historical and/or famous, or just someone whose head you're interested in climbing into.

In **third person**, a narrator tells us the story and refers to the main character by name or as "he" or "she." For example:

> *Kenny's life had been weird for ten years,*
> *three months, and eleven days. He didn't*
> *spend time worrying about it. It was just*
> *the way his life was.*

You have practiced writing in third person many times in your notebook. In doing the "people-watching" exercise on page 26, for example, you gained experience in third-person writing.

Sometimes a writer will shift from the point of view of one character to another. The reader learns the thoughts and feelings of more than one character this way. But it's tricky to do.

Use this exercise to practice writing from the point of view of more than one character:

You have probably been in a class when students are giving a substitute teacher a hard time.

First, describe the scene from the point of view of a student troublemaker.

Next, write about the situation from the point of view of the substitute teacher, as if you were that person.

Finally, write from the point of view of a student in the class who is the child of that substitute.

Your three different points of view should be interesting.

(Experiment with this exercise by writing both in first person and in third. Find out which feels more comfortable for each situation.)

Write about Mother's Day from these points of view:

☆ A child making a Mother's Day art project in school

☆ The mother of the child who made the art project

☆ A woman who works in a Hallmark store whose mother has died

_____

_____

_____

_____

_____

_____

_____

_____

_____

_____

_____

_____

_____

_____

Think of a story that has a character readers don't root for. For example: Captain Hook in *Peter Pan*, Miss Hannigan in *Annie*, Darth Vader in *Star Wars*. Try writing a scene from this character's point of view. How does this change the story?

_____

_____

_____

_____

_____

_____

_____

_____

_____

_____

_____

_____

_____

_____

_____

_____

_____

Finally, when someone is said to be "hawk-eyed" it means that the person has the keen, sharp vision of a hawk. Suppose you actually *are* a hawk, gliding over a meadow and diving for your prey. Describe this, using a hawk's point of view.

_____

_____

_____

_____

_____

_____

_____

_____

_____

_____

_____

_____

_____

_____

_____

_____

_____

Dialogue

Now, *this* is fun! If you like to talk, you'll like dialogue. It's when characters speak to one another. You'll probably like it even if you're not a big talker, because it's a different way to express yourself. And you don't have to feel self-conscious.

For many readers, dialogue is the most entertaining part of the story. Strong dialogue is important in letting your readers know details about your characters' thoughts and actions. The trick is to make it sound natural, while at the same time you pack it full of information: thoughts, feelings, reactions, body language, relationships.

Listen when you hear a conversation. (Yes, it's a bit like eavesdropping, but it's for a good cause.) Pay attention to the rhythm and patterns of speech.

When you write dialogue, you're making it possible for your reader to "hear" what's going on. It's good to read your dialogue aloud to be sure it sounds the way you want it to.

You can practice writing dialogue by having a pretend conversation with someone you've never met but would like to talk with. Tip: When you write dialogue, start a new paragraph each time a different person speaks. This helps the reader know who's saying what.

You want the reader to know not only who is saying what but *how* they are saying it. This is where body language comes in. For example: Is it being said excitedly? Angrily? With a hand on the hip? Under his breath? Tapping a fingernail on the desk?

Another way to practice writing dialogue is to just "drop into" a situation and have the characters interact. Make up a scene such as:

"You what? You walked out of science class?" Jenny exclaimed, her eyes wide with surprise.

"Yup, I'd had it. Couldn't take it anymore," I answered. "So when Mr. Yaz turned to write on the board, I just got up and left."

Jenny stared, her mouth wide open. Then she shook her head and said, "Mike, it's your funeral."

You could continue, telling what happened next as more people heard what went on in science class.

Try your own scene using lots of dialogue.

_____

_____

_____

_____

_____

_____

_____

Plot

"The plot is the reason for the story."
— Newbery Medal author Elizabeth Yates,
in her book, *Someday You'll Write*

Plot and character go together like peanut butter and jelly, like milk and cookies, and like Mickey and Minnie.

What the main character wants — and how he or she goes about getting it — is the basis for your plot. Struggles and obstacles along the way make it interesting and pull the reader along.

When you plot a story, you generally begin by introducing the characters and letting the reader know about the setting — where and when the story is taking place. The main character's problem is revealed, and you'll then make the character's struggle to solve the problem difficult by putting obstacles in his or her way. There will finally be a big moment, or climax, in the story. It's the "turning point" in the story's action. The story winds down as the problems are worked out.

Think of a few stories you know and write down the plots (in simple form, not in great detail).

Next, trying plotting an idea that you have for a story.

What keeps readers turning pages? **Worry, tension**, and **suspense**! We want to root for a struggling character, we want to know if the problem will be solved — simply, we want to know what happens next.

Keep the pace moving. Carry the reader along. Stick to the important things. You can skip the blowing of the nose, the emptying of the wastepaper basket, and the trips to the bathroom. Just tell the reader what's important to the story.

Think about some fast-paced, suspense-filled stories that you've liked. Reread them and see if you can figure out how the author kept the tension so well.

☆ Can you find the "turning point" in the story's action?

☆ What writing skills are evident?

☆ Why did you want to read on?

_____

_____

_____

_____

_____

_____

_____

Theme

It's the point of the story. It's what the story illustrates through character and plot.

If you are asked to tell what your story is about in just a sentence or a phrase, and you say something such as "kindness is rewarded," you've stated the theme.

There can be more than one theme if a story has layers. Below an obvious theme, there may be another less obvious one, just as below the humor there may be seriousness. And in addition to what's obvious about characters, events, and statements, there may be other meanings. Writers can be clever.

Write down the titles of three of your favorite books and next to them write what you feel is the theme (or themes).

_____

_____

_____

_____

_____

_____

_____

Endings

Endings can be as tricky as beginnings; the two balance each other. The ending is the time when your main character solves his or her own problem and "grows" in the process.

It's nice to know how your story will end before you begin writing it, but that doesn't always happen. You may change your mind, or have several ideas for possible endings, or you may develop such strong characters that they take the story places you hadn't planned on. That's always an adventure!

You'll want to try to end your story in such a way that the reader feels "satisfied" and glad to have given both the time and emotion to "live with" your characters for a while.

There is a reason why so many people have practically memorized E.B. White's final words of *Charlotte's Web:*

"Wilbur never forgot Charlotte. Although he loved her children and grandchildren dearly, none of the new spiders ever quite took her place in his heart. She was in a class by herself. It is not often that someone comes along who is a true friend and a good writer. Charlotte was both."

Look at how some of your favorite authors end their stories and think about what makes those endings work. Make a list of these excellent endings.

First drafts

The first copy of what you're working on is meant to be rough. It's a "sloppy copy." It isn't supposed to be perfect.

Professional writers do not write beautiful first drafts — nor do they worry about it. You shouldn't, either.

The point of a first draft is to get the words and ideas down. Later you can go back and fix it.

Rewriting

Yes, rewriting. It's important and it's necessary. At first, it may seem hard to imagine changing a single pearly word or golden phrase, but once you see how much better your writing becomes as you rewrite, you'll tackle it automatically. All serious writers are rewriters. Join the fellowship!

Sometimes it helps to put your first draft away for a while before revising. This is the "cooling-down period." Then come back to it with "fresh eyes." It won't be only the weak spots that will show up; the strong writing will shine through.

Your rewriting period is a chance to look at:

☆ Word choice (Do you have the best word you can think of to capture the image?)

☆ Pace (Is your story slowing down too much in spots?)

☆ Characterization (Is your character developing into someone the reader will care about?)

You might find a fellow writer to look at your work. When you ask a reader to help edit, be sure to discuss with this person what *does* work well, not only what *doesn't* work well.

It's in the rewriting that the true story emerges, the same way a beautiful statue is born from a chunk of rock.

To be a good writer, you must be a reader.

Writers learn from reading. Read as often as you can. Being a writer will change the way you read. You'll start paying attention to how other writers make that connection between the reader and what's put down on the pages.

Reread your favorite books.

Take your time and slowly examine them.
Next to their titles, write down what it is that makes them work:

- ☆ How does the author grip you?

- ☆ What makes you care about the characters?

- ☆ How is the story paced?

- ☆ What does the author do to create a satisfying ending?

- ☆ What has made you remember and love the book?

_____

_____

_____

_____

_____

_____

_____

_____

_____

Writing to an author

You may admire an author so much that you'd like to write to him or her. Because authors' addresses are private, you should mail your letter to the author by way of the author's publisher, who will then send it along to the author. The address of the publisher can be found on the copyright page of the author's book.

Address the envelope like this:

Author's name
c/o Publisher
Publisher's address

Illustrations

Should you illustrate your writing? If you have artistic ability, by all means add illustrations. They can add a great deal. But keep in mind that your words must be strong enough to stand alone.

Illustrations have an effect upon how the book is viewed and upon what age reader it will appeal to. Some books need no illustrations, others need just a few, and still others work best with a generous amount. The mood of the book will be affected by the illustrations. Serious, sophisticated oil paintings will help set the tone of a book in one way, while lighthearted cartoon drawings will make a very different impression. Take a look at several illustrated books, such as these suggested below, and consider the role played by the illustrations:

Winnie the Pooh by A. A. Milne
Madeline by Ludwig Bemelmans
Where the Wild Things Are by Maurice Sendak
How the Grinch Stole Christmas by Dr. Seuss
The Very Hungry Caterpillar by Eric Carle
The Polar Express by Chris Van Allsburg
A Light in the Attic by Shel Silverstein

Getting published

Getting published is not easy but it is also not impossible. If being published is a goal of yours, be persistent and take it one step at a time.

If your class or school has publications such as a newspaper or a literary magazine, submit your work.

If your school sponsors creative writing contests, enter them.

If your community has a local newspaper, send in letters and articles.

Send your work to magazines that publish kids' writing. There is a list of such publications in the *Resources for Young Writers* section of this book.

Investigate the web sites that publish creative writing by kids. Again, check the *Resources for Young Writers* section for a list of cyber-resources.

Libraries sometimes post publishers' contests for books written by young authors. An example is the annual Publish-A-Book Contest sponsored by Raintree Steck-Vaughn for students in grades 2–5. To receive an entry form, call 1-800-531-5015. Mail your submission to:

Publish-A-Book Contest
P.O. Box 27010
Austin, TX 78755

Check with your librarian about other book publishers looking for student submissions.

Remember, to be a writer, you do not have to be published. You merely have to write, write, write. As with everything, practice will make you better.

Special note: You should *never* have to pay a fee to have your work read or published.

Stick-to-itiveness — a "must-have" quality of successful writers

Among all their other collections, most serious writers have a collection of rejection letters from publishers who decided not to publish their work. Manuscripts sometimes resemble boomerangs. They go out to publishers and fly back, and then they go out again and then fly back once more. Back and forth, back and forth.

Before it was published and won the Newbery Medal, Madeleine L'Engle's *A Wrinkle in Time* was rejected repeatedly. And even the beloved Dr. Seuss faced disappointment. *And to Think That I Saw It on Mulberry Street* was turned down twenty-eight times!

So if you're serious about writing, and you'd eventually like to see your work in print, you'll have to acquire "stick-to-itiveness" and not take no for an answer.

Writing classes

Keep a lookout for writing classes, not just in school but in the community. Many local educational services offer classes for kids. Sometimes libraries, bookstores, and recreation departments sponsor writing classes.

Writing groups and clubs

Some enthusiastic writers find other writers who live nearby and form a group. The group meets to discuss writing, talk about writing news, and respond to one another's writing. These groups can be wonderful. They are a chance to get to know other writers and to learn from, and with, them.

It is important to always remember that the point of the group is to encourage and support. It's not about attacking someone's ideas, leaving the writer discouraged. Competition is not part of it. Instead, the group is for sharing the process of writing and for helping fellow writers improve their craft.

If this appeals to you, think about starting a group. You may end up with some of the closest friends you'll ever have.

The writing doesn't stop here.

When you've filled the pages of this book, get another. And another. Use your notebooks until they are filled and worn.

Feel free to redo exercises from this notebook. Much of what you did will eventually become second-nature and automatic. You'll become an expert observer and "idea catcher."

If you make it a habit to keep a writer's notebook, you will find that you not only learn and observe a lot about others, but you will also learn much about yourself. Your notebook will become a trusted friend. Writing is a way of keeping yourself company. Don't be surprised if you find that some of your best moments are just between you and your notebook.

Writing Terms

Body Language Facial expressions, tone of voice, gestures, and other physical actions that add to our knowledge of a character.

Character A person in a story or play.

Character Development The evolution of qualities and personality traits of a character.

Dialogue What the characters say to one another.

First-person Viewpoint A character, usually the main character, tells the story using the pronoun "I."

Manuscript A copy of an author's written work, usually handwritten or typed and unbound.

Motive A reason for a character's behavior.

Narrator The person who is telling the story.

Plot The series of actions and incidents, one building upon the next, as the main character struggles with his or her problem(s).

Point of View Where the story is coming from and who is telling it.

Setting The place and time of the story.

Show, Don't Tell The writer shows the story unfolding, allowing the reader to "be there," rather than merely telling the reader what happened without letting the reader experience it.

Theme The point of the story, illustrated through character and plot.

Third-person Viewpoint A narrator tells the story. Characters are referred to by name and by the pronouns "he" and "she."

Resources for Young Writers

BOOKS

Asher, Sandy. *Where Do You Get Your Ideas?* New York: Walker & Company, 1987.
Writing suggestions and encouragement from Sandy Asher, as well as from many other children's book authors.

Asher, Sandy. *Wild Words! How to Train Them to Tell Stories.* New York: Walker & Company, 1989.
Tips for young writers on how to use language to create vivid characters and gripping plots.

Bauer, Marion Dane. *What's Your Story? A Young Person's Guide to Writing Fiction.* New York: Clarion Books, 1992.
A helpful guide that explores what it takes to write fiction. The author covers such key topics as plot, character, point of view, dialogue, keeping the reader hooked, and revision.

Children's Writer's & Illustrator's Market. Cincinnati: Writer's Digest Books. Published annually.
This reference tool includes a section called "Young Writer's and Illustrator's Market," which lists many publications seeking materials by kids.

Dahlstrom, Lorraine M. *Writing Down the Days: 365 Creative Journaling Ideas for Young People*. Minneapolis: Free Spirit Publishing, 1990.
A full year of journal-writing ideas, along with interesting facts about each day of the year. Many entries include names and addresses for further information.

Fletcher, Ralph. *A Writer's Notebook: Unlocking the Writer Within You*. New York: Avon Books, 1996.
This guide shows young writers the importance of a writer's notebook as a writing tool and as "a place to live like a writer."

Fox, Nancy. *The Writer's Notebook: Ideas for Creative Writing and Self-Expression*. Santa Barbara: The Learning Works, 1998.
Designed for students in grades 5—8, this book helps young writers answer the question, "What shall I write about?" It includes sections on essays, poetry, research, and stories.

Henderson, Kathy. *Market Guide for Young Writers*. Cincinnati: Writer's Digest Books. Published annually.
If you're hoping to become published, this guide will help you learn about magazines, publishers, and contests featuring kids' writing.

Naylor, Phyllis Reynolds. *How I Came to Be a Writer*.
New York: Aladdin Books, 1987.
Newbery Award—winning author Phyllis Reynolds
Naylor tells her story and shares background infor-
mation on many of her books.

Wilber, Jessica. *Totally Private and Personal Journaling
Ideas for Girls and Young Women*. Minneapolis: Free
Spirit Publishing, 1996.
The fourteen-year-old author provides writing tips,
journal ideas, and advice. She also lists other helpful
resources.

MAGAZINES

(Submissions may be sent to the addresses listed.)

American Girl. 8400 Fairway Place, Middleton, WI
53562.
Publishes writing of eight- to twelve-year-olds.

Creative Kids. P.O. Box 8813, Waco, TX 76714.
Contains stories, poetry, artwork, opinion, photog-
raphy, and games by kids ages eight to fourteen.

Girls' Life. 4517 Harford Road, Baltimore, MD 21214.
Welcomes letters, provides pen-pal listings, and includes book and film reviews.

Highlights for Children. 803 Church Street, Honesdale, PA 18431.
Features writing of kids through age fifteen.

Merlyn's Pen: The National Magazine of Student Writing. P.O. Box 1058, East Greenwich, RI 02818.
There is a middle school edition (for writers in grades 6–9) as well as a high school edition for older student writers.

New Moon: The Magazine for Girls and Their Dreams. P.O. Box 3620, Duluth, MN 55803.
Girls ages eight to fourteen edit this magazine and accept contributions from girls all over the world. Not supported by paid advertising.

Skipping Stones. P.O. Box 3939, Eugene, OR 97403.
The emphasis is upon multicultural and environmental pieces.

Stone Soup, The Magazine by Young Writers and Artists. Children's Art Foundation, P.O. Box 83, Santa Cruz, CA 95063.
This magazine publishes fiction, poetry, and artwork by kids up to age thirteen.

WEB SITES

This list of varied and changing sites is intended as a guide to the many cyber-resources for and by creative kids. Search terms include: *creative writing for kids, writing by kids,* and *kids' writing.*

Be True http://www.betruezine.com/
   Designed for ages ten to fourteen, this on-line magazine is a place to explore and share art and writing.

Children's Express http://www.ce.org/
   A news service produced by kids. Submissions welcomed.

Children's Writings http://www.acs.ucalgary.ca/~dkbrown/writings.html
   A list of web sites featuring kids' writing.

Creative Writing for Kids http://www.kidswriting.miningco.com/
   Contains much information about writing and provides a place for young writers to submit their work.

Cyberkids http://www.cyberkids.com/
   A cyber-corner featuring kids' writing, art, and musical compositions.

Kidpub http://www.kidpub.org/kidpub/
  Kids are encouraged to submit creative writing and news stories.

Kidworld http://www.bconnex.net/~kidworld/
  Stories and jokes by kids under sixteen years old.

Kids Did This! Hotlist http://sln.fi.edu/tfi/hotlists/kids.html
  Student writing on all sorts of subjects.

KidStuff http://www.kidstuff.org/
  A "by kids/for kids" place for you to submit poems and stories and read what other kids have written.

The Little Planet Times http://www.littleplanet.com/
  Poems, stories, and artwork from kids the world over.

Midlink Magazine http://www.longwood.cs.ucf.edu/midLink/
  A digital magazine for and by kids in the middle and upper grades. Accepts stories and poems.

Stone Soup http://www.stonesoup.com/
  An Internet introduction to this magazine by young artists and writers.

Young Authors Workshop http://www.planet.eon.net/~bplaroch/publish.html

Links to on-line magazines accepting stories, articles, and poems by young writers. Writing contests are included.

Many authors have web pages and some offer tips on writing. Judy Blume, for example, has a helpful home page:

Judy Blume's Home Base
http://www.judyblume.com/home.html

Try a web search for your favorite writers and see what you can learn.

Some search services offer a web guide just for kids. *Yahooligans*, part of Yahoo, is an example. This service will help you find places that focus upon student writing. Try typing *kids' writing.*